Word Thinker Sheets

by
Becky Daniel

illustrated by Nancee McClure

Cover by Nancee McClure

ISBN No. 0-86653-394-X

Printing No. 98765

GOOD APPLE, INC.
BOX 299
CARTHAGE, IL 62321-0299

Dedication

For my late grandmother, Ann Mier, whose warm words, like sunshine, helped me grow.

Table of Contents

Patterns . . . 1
Simple Phrases . . . 2
Remove One . . . 3
Word Towers . . . 4
Gals and Lads . . . 5
Mix and Match Proverbs . . . 6
Sky High . . . 7
Sentence Fun . . . 8
Who Is It? . . . 9
Antonym Phrases . . . 10
Throw One Out! . . . 11
Scrambled Eggs . . . 12
Once Again . . . 13
Syllable Riddles . . . 14
Anagrams . . . 15
Rhymes . . . 16
Rhyming Chart . . . 17
Search and Circle . . . 18
Go Search! . . . 19
Alphabetical Words . . . 20
Big and Little . . . 21
Synonym Acrostics . . . 22
A Place to Dwell . . . 23
Double Letter Zoo . . . 24
Fifty Cents Worth . . . 25
Ring One Out . . . 26
Synonym Squares . . . 27
Thinker Sheet . . . 28
Figuratively Speaking . . . 29
In Your Own Words . . . 30
Letter Fun . . . 31
Animal Parade . . . 32
A Long Vacation . . . 33
Hidden Girls and Boys . . . 34
Associations . . . 35
Brain Strain . . . 36
Fractured Nursery Rhymes . . . 37
The Jones Boys . . . 38
The Fair . . . 39
Six Cars . . . 40
Gold, Gold, Gold! . . . 41
Lunch Out . . . 42
Diamond Thief . . . 43
Picture Message . . . 44
Homonym Hunt . . . 45
Anagrams Anyone? . . . 46
Building a Monastery . . . 47
Can It Be? . . . 48
Teatime . . . 49
Spoonerism . . . 50
Color Your Words . . . 51
Where Are You From? . . . 52
Scrambled Sayings . . . 53
Vowels Needed! . . . 54
Create Your Own Chart . . . 55
Answer Key . . . 56
Award Certificates . . . 59

To the Teacher

Word Thinker Sheets is designed to give students' minds a real workout! Children will learn the meanings of hundreds of new words when they tackle these exciting and motivating puzzles. The wide range of activities, from simple to complex, gives learners concrete practice in relational and proportional reasoning and helps them see patterns, relationships and analogies.

Most children are involved in learning based on memorizing facts rather than higher thinking skills such as application, analysis, synthesis, and evaluation. The activities in this book require children to THINK, use their imaginations and dictionaries while learning to apply rules, methods, principles and theories to new materials. The learning outcome represents a higher intellectual level than comprehension and application because students are required to understand both the content and the structural form of the material. The complexity of most of the activities makes dictionary work a must. Children should be encouraged to use their dictionaries while completing activities.

Each page contains a bonus. These activities are usually very difficult and should not be a requirement. Use the bonus activities for extra credit. A student who successfully completes one of these should receive special recognition. A class competition could involve keeping track of how many bonuses are completed by each student and rewarding those that complete a given number. Awards are found on pages 59 and 60 and a special award certificate for bonuses is included.

An answer key is provided; however, since very often the puzzles are open-ended, the answer key will only provide a list of possible answers. For many activity pages, learners will have their own unique list of answers. Discussion of alternative answers should be encouraged. If time allows, have the children follow up each activity page by creating their own puzzles.

Patterns

Look at each row of letters. Decide what pattern is used to form the chain of letters. Write the letter that follows in each row.

For example: A E I O. The letter *U* would follow because the pattern used is the vowels in alphabetical order.

1. B D F H J L __
2. B F J P __
3. A C F J O __
4. B C D G J O P Q __
5. A F H K N __

Make up your own letter pattern and write it here.

Name________________________

Bonus: Can you think of a ten-letter word that can be written using only the top row of letters on a typewriter?

Simple Phrases

In the sentences found below, words or phrases have been replaced with synonyms. Change the appropriate words or phrases and you will have famous quotations.

For example: Propel, propel, propel your ship is one way to say, "Row, row, row your boat."

1. Depart or proceed, to the carnivorous domesticated mammals. ____________

   ____

2. Possess a cutting tool, to reduce to powder by friction. ____________

   ____

3. Cover with coloring material, the center of populated area, a shade of ruby.

   ____

4. Nip or grind with teeth, the fine dry pulverized particles of earth. ____________

   ____

5. Joint in the middle of the leg, tall, to a leaping insect. ____________

   ____

Make up your own complicated sentence for a simple phrase.

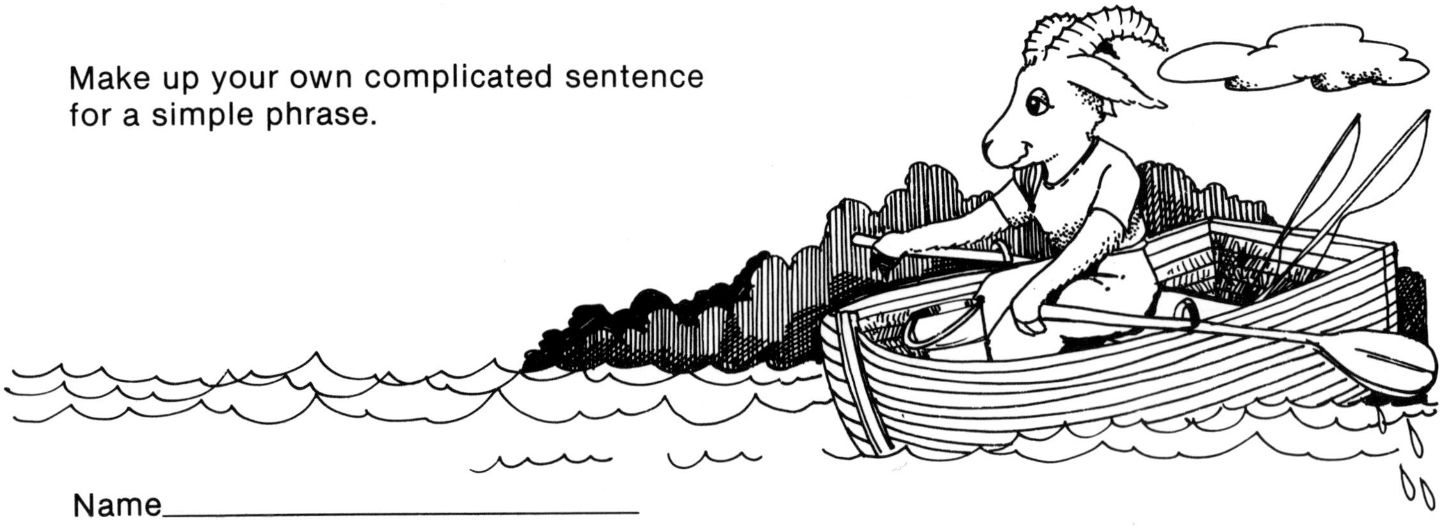

Name______________________

Bonus: Write your own complicated sentence that means, "A weed is a flower in disguise." Use at least a dozen words, more if you can.

Remove One

Each row of letters found below is the letters of two words scrambled. A clue is given for each word.

Example: Remove a city and leave the state.

Answer: Boston, Texas

1. Remove the girl and leave the boy.
   A J M A R K Y C

   ____________ ____________

2. Remove the animal and leave its baby.
   E S C H O O L R T

   ____________ ____________

3. Remove the furniture and leave the room.
   I E C H K H I R T A C N

   ____________ ____________

4. Remove the day and leave the month.
   D T S U M E A A Y Y

   ____________ ____________

5. Remove the boy and leave his toy.
   B R B E L A O A L Y S

   ____________ ____________

6. Remove the vegetable and leave the flower.
   N R C E O S R O

   ____________ ____________

Name________________________

Bonus: What profession has three double letters in succession?

Name________________________

Word Towers

Can you build a word tower? Begin by looking at the letter in the top square of each tower. Repeat the letter used in the top square and add one new letter to spell a two-letter word. Continue adding a letter to each row as you work down. Each row must spell a word. You may add the new letter at the beginning, the end, or in the middle of the word.

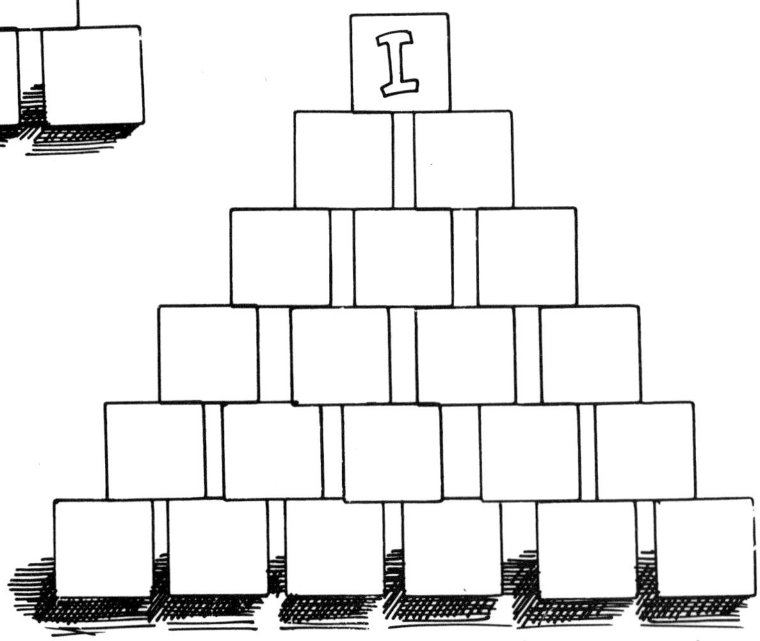

Bonus: Reverse the word tower and begin with the word *sprint*. Drop a letter leaving a word in each row until you reach a one-letter word at the top of your tower.

Gals and Lads

The answers to the riddles found below are words that begin with the three letters *gal*.

1. What gal shines and twinkles at night?

   ____

2. What gal is a party?

   ____

3. What gal holds precious art objects?

   ____

4. What gal is a famous scientist?

   ____

5. What gal means lots and lots to every-one?

   ____

The answers to the riddles found below are words that begin with the three letters *lad*.

1. What lad isn't a boy at all?

   ____

2. What lad can you step on?

   ____

3. What lad has spots and can fly?

   ____

4. What lad can you dip in your soup?

   ____

5. What lad is much too big and heavy?

   ____

Name______________________________

Bonus: What gal would you wear on your feet? What lad, although a slipper, would you never put on your feet?

Mix and Match Proverbs

Each phrase found in the left-hand column can be matched with a phrase in the right-hand column to make a famous quotation. Draw lines to match the phrases and form quotations.

1. A rolling stone	a. he tries
2. Anyone can hold the helm when	b. than never
3. No one knows what he can do till	c. a great slavery
4. It is better to learn late	d. what they seem
5. Prosperity makes friends,	e. gathers no moss
6. There is no great genius without some	f. the sea is calm
7. A great fortune is	g. adversity tries them
8. Things are not always	h. touch of madness
9. Give me where to stand, and I will	i. revolution and crime
10. Manner, not gold, is a woman's	j. craftsmanship
11. Criticism comes easier than	k. best adornment
12. Poverty is the parent of	l. move the earth
13. There is no place more delightful	m. to keep your mind even
14. Remember when life's path is steep	n. than money
15. A good reputation is more valuable	o. than home

Name______________________________

Bonus: Unscramble the words found below to spell a proverb.
heWn a dneifr akss, eethr si on ooorrmwt.

Name______________________________

Sky High

Write a word that rhymes with *sky* for each letter of the alphabet found below. Remember, rhyming words do not always end in the same letters.

Example: *Pie* is a rhyming word for *sky*.

a ____________________

b ____________________

c ____________________

d ____________________

e ____________________

f ____________________

g ____________________

h ____________________

i ____________________

j ____________________

k ____________________

l ____________________

m ____________________

n ____________________

o ____________________

p ____________________

q ____________________

r ____________________

s ____________________

t ____________________

u ____________________

v ____________________

w ____________________

x ____________________

y ____________________

Bonus: Unscramble the letters found below to make two words that rhyme with *sky*. Hint: One word is a month of the year.

i j l l l m p t u u y y ________ ________

Name______________________________

Sentence Fun

Some letters and numbers sound like words. Each row of letters and numbers found below represents a sentence. Write each sentence.

Example: I C U = I see you.

1. O I C U. ______________________________
2. I C A B. ______________________________
3. R U J? ______________________________
4. I ½ 2 B N by 10. ______________________________
5. R U L8 2? ______________________________
6. I 1 A 10 Tcup. ______________________________
7. I C N NDN TP. ______________________________
8. M I 2 L8 2 C J? ______________________________

Sometimes a combination of letters sounds like a word. Read each clue below and think of a combination of letters that represents the one-word answer for each clue.

Example: 4 C = foresee

1. Not hard to do is__________
2. Someone that is not a friend is called an__________
3. A boy's name__________
4. Too much of something is called__________

Make a list of words that can be represented by letter combinations.

Bonus: What four-letter combination sounds like you are addressing an ambassador?

Who Is It?

The small words in each line below are the names of famous people. Unscramble each line of words and write the name of each famous person on the appropriate line.

Example: peek as shear = Shakespeare

1. oh, sing want ______
2. seen it in ______
3. the oven be ______
4. at some dish, no ______ ______
5. he try pin rack ______ ______
6. then jams rose off ______ ______

Use this space to write a famous person's name. Scramble the letters into small words.

Use this space to write small words and scramble the name of a friend?

Name______

Bonus: Rearrange some of the words in the sentence found below so that it means the opposite. You may not add or leave out any words.

I looked over the newspaper this morning.

Antonym Phrases

One or two words in each phrase found below has been replaced with an antonym. If you replace the correct words with antonyms you will discover some famous phrases.

1. Fly on the handle ______________________________
2. Give tabs off ______________________________
3. Bark down the right tree ______________________________
4. Hold the doe ______________________________
5. Uncover the hatchet ______________________________
6. It will drop water. ______________________________

Think of some familiar phrases and replace some of the words with antonyms to make your own antonym phrases.

Name______________________________

Bonus: Each word in the sentence found below is an antonym for the actual word in a famous phrase. Change each word to rewrite the phrase.

Injustice isn't lies out motionlessness.

Throw One Out!

Each line contains four words. Read the words and think about how they are related. One word in each row doesn't belong. Cross out the word in each row that doesn't go with the others. On the line under each row, explain what the other three words have in common.

1. onion potato tomato carrot

   ____

2. square triangle rectangle circle

   ____

3. basketball marbles dice baseball

   ____

4. hen pig horse rabbit

   ____

5. pumpkin carrot tomato yam

   ____

6. book purse tree closet

   ____

Name______________________

Bonus: Change only the punctuation in the sentence found below so that the new sentence you write means exactly the opposite.

Private! No children allowed.

Scrambled Eggs

Unscramble the two lists of words below. Then draw a line connecting each word to a homonyn, antonym or synonym.

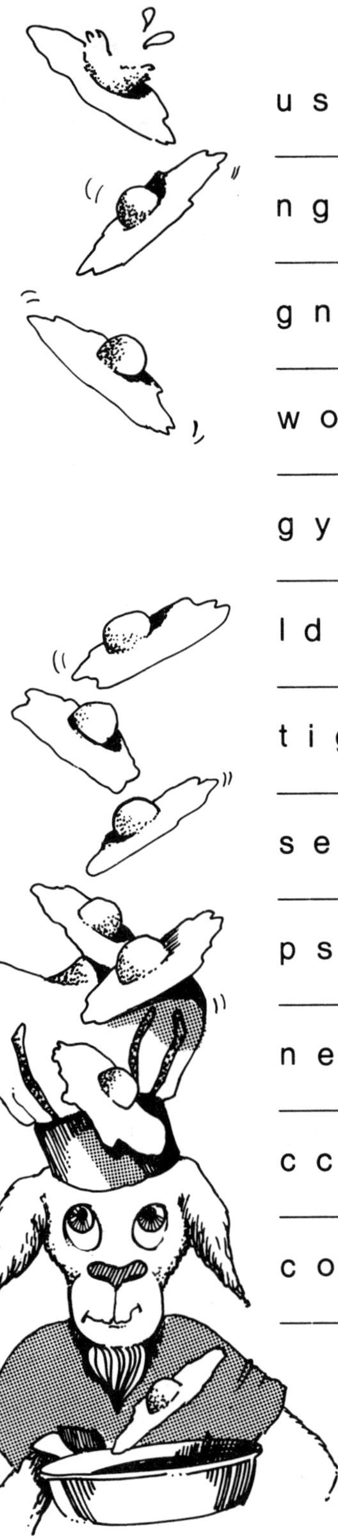

1. n a r i ____________
2. g e s e d s u ____________
3. g t h n i ____________
4. g s h o u b ____________
5. o k d e r o c ____________
6. b u e a i f t l u ____________
7. g u o n y ____________
8. w k a e a ____________
9. d u l i b ____________
10. a e l b m ____________
11. a e e n d r m ____________
12. t e o t ____________

u s e g t ____________

n g t h i k ____________

g n e i r ____________

w o s b ____________

g y u l ____________

l d o ____________

t i g h r a s t ____________

s e a e p l ____________

p s n o r t t a r ____________

n e r w a d ____________

c c s e a u ____________

c o t u t c r s n ____________

Name____________________

Bonus: Make a list of twenty-five animal words that have homonyms. Write the homonym for each animal on your list. Example: *ant, aunt*

Once Again

All the words of famous sayings are given below but not in the correct order. Unscramble the words in each sentence and write the quotation correctly.

1. The boundary is not the world of the horizon.

2. Evil, evil, evil, see speak hear, no no no.

3. Hard success is the work of secret.

4. Servant is a good master but poor a money.

5. The lies prize in the virtue struggle not in the.

6. Not want waste not.

7. Question is that the be not be to or to.

Scramble the words of one of your favorite sayings.

Name________________________

Bonus: Unscramble the words below to spell a proverb.

oYu nacton aekm na eeltom ithwotu aeibrkng gges.

Syllable Riddles

The answer to each of the riddles found below is broken into syllables. A clue is given for each syllable. Write your answers on the lines under each clue.

Example: Something found at the end of your leg + a dancing party = football.

1. The name of one planet and a trembling movement are what kind of disaster?

   _______ + _______ = _______

2. A baseball glove and a number between one and twelve are what piece of winter wear?

   _______ + _______ = _______

3. A letter of the alphabet and a girl's hair ribbon make what part of the body?

   _______ + _______ = _______

4. To twirl around and to mix with a spoon are what kind of person?

   _______ + _______ = _______

5. To brush with a broom and a special cut of beef are what kind of contest?

   _______ + _______ = _______

Name_______________________

Bonus: When is getting a blow to the face with the palm of a hand and a thin piece of wood funny?

Anagrams

Each of the words listed below contains letters that can be arranged to spell another word. Write a new word by unscrambling the letters in each word found below.

Name______________________________

Bonus: What four-letter word can be rearranged to spell four other words?

Rhymes

1. What word rhymes with "geese" and means heavy? ________
2. What word rhymes with "meek" and means very old and valuable? ________
3. What word rhymes with "great" and means merrymaking? ________
4. What word rhymes with "fine" and means to plan something? ________
5. What word rhymes with "wise" and means to make use of? ________
6. What word rhymes with "slow" and is used to make bread? ________
7. What word rhymes with "bear" and means to rip? ________
8. What word rhymes with "wag" and means short, sharp turns? ________
9. What word rhymes with "yell" and means to outdo? ________

Bonus: Below are clues for five different words. The answers will all rhyme.

to chatter ________

a kind of sour apple ________

to strike or touch gently ________

dull brownish color ________

to snatch ________

Name________________________________

Rhyming Chart

Complete the chart found below. Each row of words must rhyme. Each column of words must fit the category listed at the top of the column. Some of the chart has been filled in for you.

			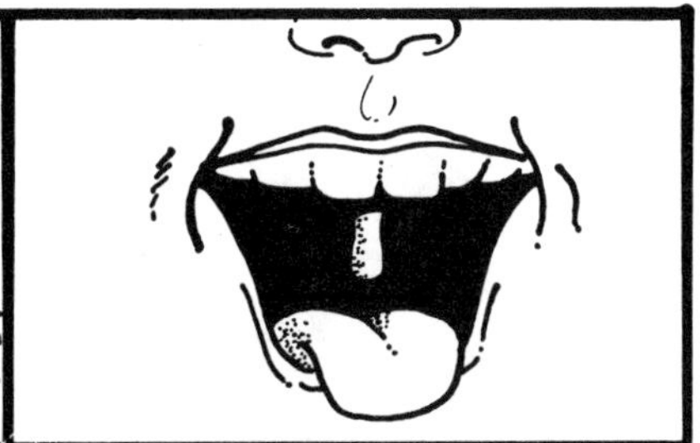
	Animal	**Plant**	**Sound**
am	*ram*		
dill			*shrill*
nine		*pine*	
tape			
air			

Name________________________________

Bonus: Make a list of eight animals that have rhyming animal partners. Example: *lice, mice*

Search and Circle

In each row of letters found below are two antonyms. Find and circle the antonyms in each row. Then use this puzzle format to design three antonym puzzles of your own.

1. r b o p p o s e e x c o m p l y e s o o n
2. d i s c o n t i n u e b i c e a s e a d d
3. b y s e i z e p r e l e a s e e n d i v e
4. e s e r e n e a d d i s t u r b e d f o r
5.
6.
7.

In each row of letters found below are two synonyms. Find and circle the synonyms in each row. Then create three synonym puzzles of your own.

1. p o o r s c a r c e r a r e a d o e p n x
2. b i h a s t y e s e a s u d d e n o t e p
3. d o s w e l l a w e x p a n d i v i d e t
4. c o a r s e d i n a p r o u g h l l e w s
5.
6.
7.

Bonus: What are two rhyming antonyms for the word *mix*?

Name________________________

Go Search!

Can you list thirteen words hidden in the line of letters found below? You do not have to rearrange any letters.

s t r a i n p i r a t e s

1. ______________ 8. ______________
2. ______________ 9. ______________
3. ______________ 10. ______________
4. ______________ 11. ______________
5. ______________ 12. ______________
6. ______________ 13. ______________
7. ______________

Can you find thirteen words hidden in the line below? Again, you do not have to rearrange any letters.

s p i n s t e r t u r n i p s

1. ______________ 8. ______________
2. ______________ 9. ______________
3. ______________ 10. ______________
4. ______________ 11. ______________
5. ______________ 12. ______________
6. ______________ 13. ______________
7. ______________

Name______________________________

Bonus: Somewhere on this page there is a mispelled word. Bonus points awarded to the genius that finds it!

Alphabetical Words

How many words can you list that have every letter in alphabetical order?

Example: a**b**cdefghijk**l**mn**o**pqrs**t**uvwxyz = blot

1. ______________
2. ______________
3. ______________
4. ______________
5. ______________
6. ______________
7. ______________
8. ______________
9. ______________
10. ______________
11. ______________
12. ______________
13. ______________
14. ______________
15. ______________
16. ______________
17. ______________
18. ______________
19. ______________
20. ______________
21. ______________
22. ______________
23. ______________
24. ______________
25. ______________
26. ______________
27. ______________
28. ______________
29. ______________
30. ______________
31. ______________
32. ______________
33. ______________
34. ______________
35. ______________
36. ______________
37. ______________
38. ______________
39. ______________
40. ______________
41. ______________
42. ______________
43. ______________
44. ______________
45. ______________
46. ______________
47. ______________
48. ______________
49. ______________
50. ______________

Name______________________________

Bonus: Can you think of a flower that has a rhyming bird?

Big and Little

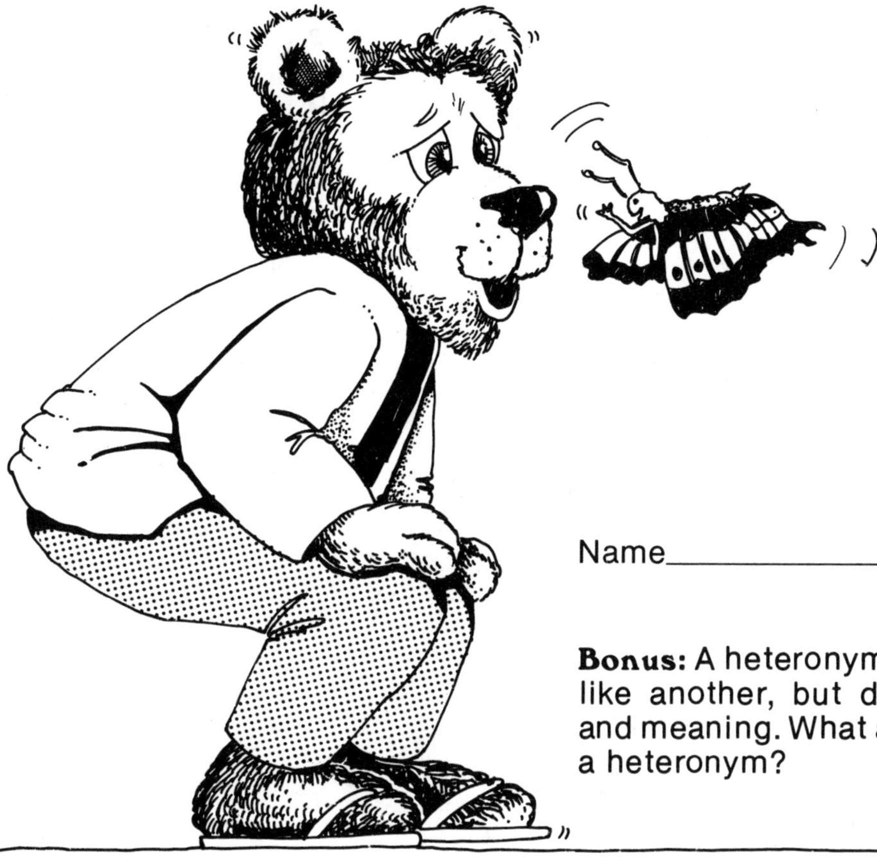

Name________________________________

Bonus: A heteronym is a word spelled like another, but differing in sound and meaning. What antonym for *big* is a heteronym?

Ten synonyms for the word *big* are listed below. The words are divided and the lists scrambled. Draw a line connecting the letters that spell synonyms for *big.*

1. l a r	a s t
2. e x t e n	g e
3. v	m e n s e
4. i m	s i v e
5. e n o r	m o u s
6. t r e	t i c
7. h	m e n d o u s
8. m a s	u g e
9. g i g a n	m o t h
10. m a m	s i v e

Unscramble the words below. Then list them in order from the smallest to the largest.

1. e k w e ________ ________
2. y d a ________ ________
3. d e o c n s ________ ________
4. h o t m n ________ ________
5. i e u m n t ________ ________
6. n s s e a o ________ ________
7. a e y r ________ ________
8. v e e i g n n ________ ________
9. e e a d d c ________ ________
10. y t e u c r n ________ ________

Synonym Acrostics

Look at the word in each puzzle below. Choose synonyms for each word that has the appropriate number of letters to complete the puzzles. For example: A synonym for *change* that begins with the letter *C* and has seven letters is *convert*. So write *convert* in the line of the first puzzle.

Name____________________________

Bonus: Can you think of two synonyms for *disaster* that rhyme?

A Place to Dwell

In the letter maze below are hidden eleven places to dwell. The words may be written in a straight line or have one angle. They may be written down or across. You must use every letter in the maze to spell the eleven dwellings, and no letter is used more than once. One of the eleven is circled for you.

d	u	p	l	c	a
c	h	t	e	h	v
a	u	e	x	o	e
s	t	n	t	t	c
t	l	e	l	e	a
h	o	u	s	i	b
f	i	s	e	n	m
a	g	l	o	o	a
r	m	w	i	g	w

Bonus: Add a letter in front of and after the two small words *on* and *do* to spell a place you could live.

ondo

Name____________________

Double Letter Zoo

Many animals have double letters in their names. Can you complete this list of animal names with double letters in them?

Example: LL_ _ _ = llama

1. _ _ _ _LL_

2. _ _ _ _LL_

3. _ _ _ _RR_ _

4. _OO_ _

5. _OO_ _

6. _ _FF_ _ _

7. _ _ _ _FF_

8. _ _PP_ _ _ _ _ _ _ _

9. _ _ _SS_ _

10. _ _BB_ _

11. _ _ _ _ _EE_

Name________________________

Bonus: What animal can be spelled by putting two color words together and changing only one vowel to another vowel?

Fifty Cents Worth

On each coin below, write a word that rhymes with *cent*.

Name____________________________

Bonus: List two homonyms that rhyme with *cent*.

Ring One Out

Each line contains four words. Read the words and decide which three words in each row are synonyms. Cross out the word in each row that doesn't belong.

1. haughty	conceited	bad	egotistical
2. imitation	genuine	unreal	counterfeit
3. swoop	descend	drop	rise
4. pull	push	nudge	prod
5. petty	grand	trivial	inferior
6. intimidate	cow	bully	close
7. strew	beef	squander	spread
8. alarm	startle	terrible	terrorize
9. irregular	unnatural	ordinary	anomalous
10. monumental	supreme	superior	unknown
11. vanish	approach	arrive	appear
12. faith	confidence	doubt	trust
13. brag	boast	crow	hide
14. performance	exercise	idleness	operation

Name______________________________

Bonus: What word does not belong in the row of words found below? What do the other three words have in common?

enharten permote prompt encite

Synonym Squares

Choose synonyms for the clues given to complete these word squares. Then use the last word square to create your own puzzle.

1.

Down
1. burden
2. rim

Across
1. gallop
3. eat

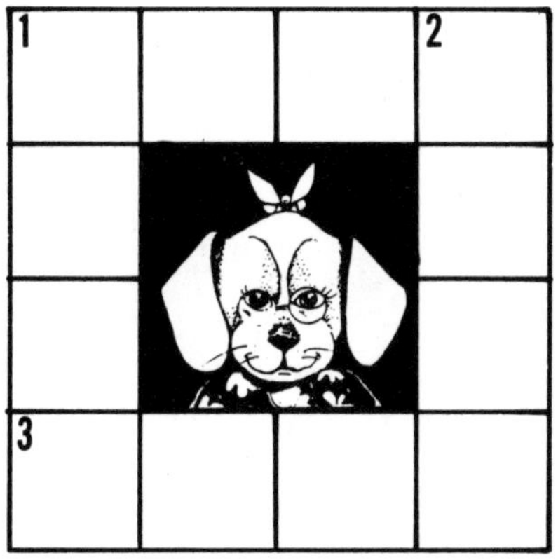

2.

Down
1. genuine
2. smooth

Across
1. unique
3. grass

3.

Down
1. illustrious
2. pull

Across
1. troop
3. consider

4.

Down
1.
2.

Across
1.
3.

Name______________________________

Bonus: Create your own homonym word square.

Thinker Sheet

1. What homonyms mean to lift, to demolish and sunbeams?

2. Can you spell four animals that rhyme?

3. Add a letter to the word *anger* and get something hazardous.

4. What eleven-letter word, beginning with the letter *P*, means the opposite of *optimistic*?

5. Can you spell a ten-letter word that begins with the letter *M* and means the opposite of *obvious*?

6. What six-letter word that rhymes with *cake* means *dark* or *obscure*?

7. What state has two homonyms meaning *hair* and *principal*?

8. Spell ten words that have a silent letter *T*.

9. Spell twelve words that begin with a silent letter *K*.

Name______________________________

Bonus: What fourteen-letter word should you never, ever lock in a dark closet?

Figuratively Speaking

Write a synonym for each bold word to discover a famous phrase.

Example: **eat** the **soil** = bite the dust

1. **skip** the **pistol** ______
2. **munch modest pastry** ______
3. **tip** the **fruit wagon** ______
4. a **moist cover** ______
5. **steal** the **dessert** ______
6. **whip** the **orchestra** ______
7. **happy** as **fruit juice** ______

Unscramble the words below to spell some other famous phrases.

Example: yfl het pooc = fly the coop

1. a lidw eoogs hscae ______
2. ot teab hte abdn ______
3. rbak pu hte rnwog rtee ______
4. lpya ceosdn ddifel ______
5. upjm eht nug ______
6. neco ni a ubel omon ______

Name______

Bonus: Each word in the phrase found below has been replaced with a synonym or a homonym. Can you rewrite the famous phrase correctly?
Greater strength two ewe.

In Your Own Words

Below are some unfinished famous quotations. Complete each quotation in your own words. After your teacher reads the endings for these famous quotations, decide how close your meanings were to the authors' original meanings. Did you come up with some sayings worth remembering?

1. He that plants thorns must ______________________
2. There are some who bear a grudge even ______________________
3. There is no greater bane to friendship than ______________________
4. Old age is by nature ______________________
5. For there is nothing more silly than ______________________
6. I have built me a monument ______________________
7. Seek for truth in the ______________________
8. Scandal has ever been ______________________
9. To be loved ______________________
10. It is a very hard undertaking to seek to please ______________________
11. It is not the man who has too little, but the man who craves more ______________________

    ____
12. A great fortune is ______________________

Name______________________

Bonus: There is a famous saying, "If I rest, I rust." Write your own saying that means almost the same thing. Can you think of one that sounds better and is more poetic than the original?

Letter Fun

Finish each letter riddle with a letter and a reason for your answer.

Example: What letter of the alphabet do we need to get married?

Answer: D, the letter *D* makes we, wed.

1. What letter of the alphabet do you want to always keep out of the freezer?

   Answer: ______ ____

2. What letter of the alphabet is the most happy?

   Answer: ______ ____

3. What letter of the alphabet is like midnight?

   Answer: ______ ____

4. What letter of the alphabet makes Dad spend a lot of money?

   Answer: ______ ____

5. What letter of the alphabet is like noon?

   Answer: ______ ____

6. What letter of the alphabet is just like Paris?

   Answer: ______ ____

7. What letter is just like the letter *Z*?

   Answer: ______ ____

Name____________________________

Bonus: What is at the beginning of eternity and at the end of time?

Animal Parade

Write a list of animals. Each animal you list must begin with the last letter of the previous animal. You may not use an animal more than once in your "parade." What is the longest parade you can form?

Example: do**g** **g**oa**t** **t**urtl**e** **e**lephant

1. ______________
2. ______________
3. ______________
4. ______________
5. ______________
6. ______________
7. ______________
8. ______________
9. ______________
10. ______________
11. ______________
12. ______________
13. ______________
14. ______________
15. ______________
16. ______________
17. ______________
18. ______________
19. ______________
20. ______________
21. ______________
22. ______________
23. ______________
24. ______________
25. ______________
26. ______________
27. ______________
28. ______________
29. ______________
30. ______________
31. ______________
32. ______________
33. ______________
34. ______________
35. ______________
36. ______________
37. ______________
38. ______________
39. ______________
40. ______________

Name______________________________

Bonus: What animal has three double letters in the word?

A Long Vacation

Write a list of places to go on vacation. Each place must begin with the last letter of the previous place. You may not visit the same place twice. What is the longest vacation you can write?

Example: Pari**s**, **S**outh Carolin**a**, **A**tlant**a**, **A**lask**a**, **A**msterdam

1. ______	11. ______	21. ______	31. ______
2. ______	12. ______	22. ______	32. ______
3. ______	13. ______	23. ______	33. ______
4. ______	14. ______	24. ______	34. ______
5. ______	15. ______	25. ______	35. ______
6. ______	16. ______	26. ______	36. ______
7. ______	17. ______	27. ______	37. ______
8. ______	18. ______	28. ______	38. ______
9. ______	19. ______	29. ______	39. ______
10. ______	20. ______	30. ______	40. ______

Name______________________

Bonus: Which two states have three double letters in them?

Hidden Girls and Boys

How many girls' names can you spell using the letters found in the letter grid below? Move from square to square. You may go left to right, right to left, upward, downward or diagonally. You may reenter a square. There are at least nine names.

U	S	J	E	N
E	H	A	M	N
J	A	R	Y	E
E	N	U	K	R
A	N	T	H	A

1. ____________
2. ____________
3. ____________
4. ____________
5. ____________
6. ____________
7. ____________
8. ____________
9. ____________

Find nine boys' names in the letter grid below.

J	N	H	O	T
R	A	J	E	R
R	A	T	N	R
Y	C	T	O	Y
E	K	I	M	E

1. ____________
2. ____________
3. ____________
4. ____________
5. ____________
6. ____________
7. ____________
8. ____________
9. ____________

Name______________________________

Bonus: Make a list of ten names that have homonyms. Example: *Abel, able*

Associations

Each line contains four words. Find a word that is associated with all four words.

1. kite office spring car
   Answer: ______________
2. market man natural highway
   Answer: ______________
3. yard load owner builder
   Answer: ______________
4. rest loose print note
   Answer: ______________
5. apple needles sap cone
   Answer: ______________
6. shine down burst bathe
   Answer: ______________

Name______________________________

Bonus: What color is associated with each word found below? ____________

elephant ______________ fish ______________ house ______________

Brain Strain

Begin in any circle. Move along the circles connected with a line. Can you find and write thirteen words that rhyme with the word *brain*?

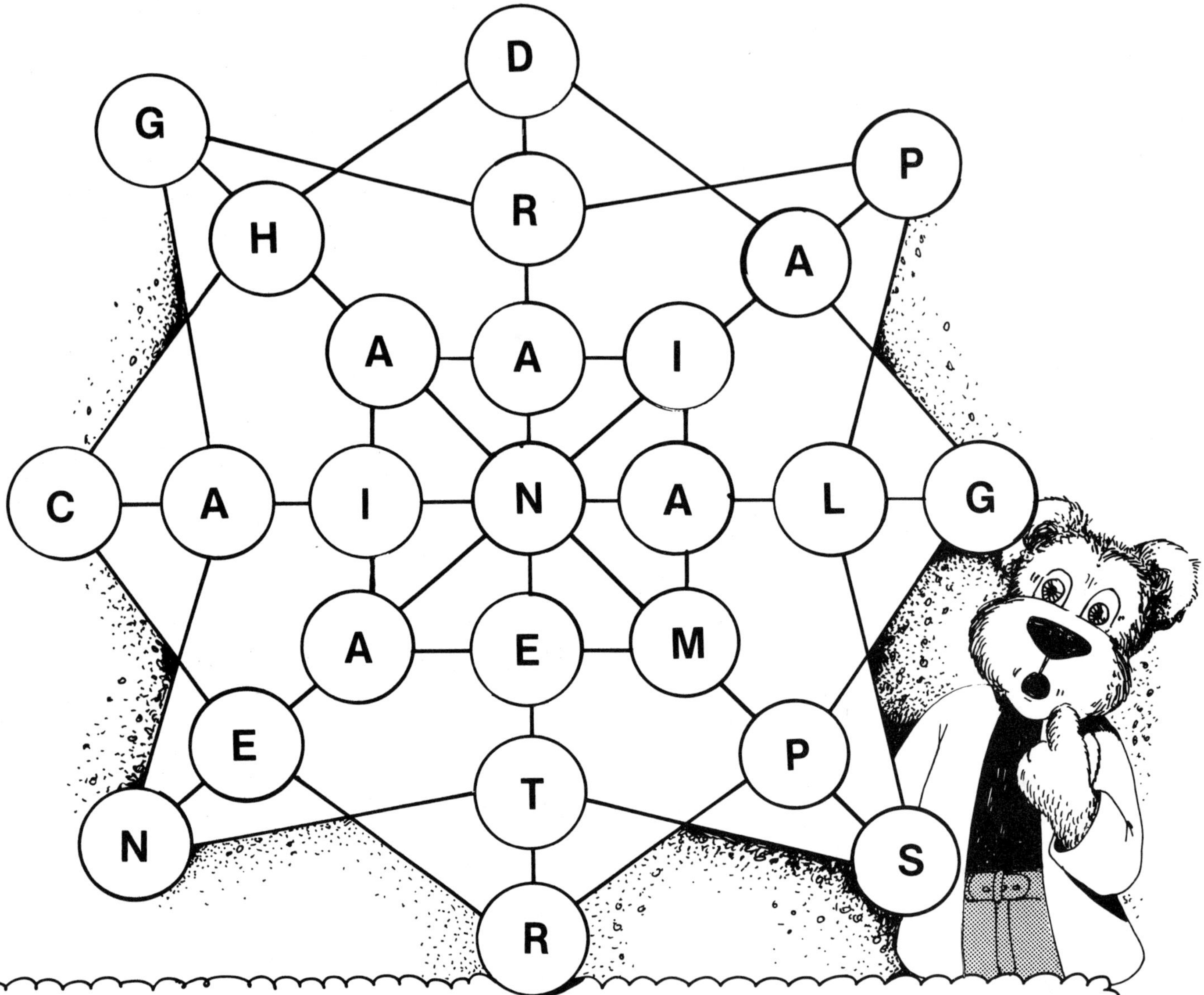

1. ____________
2. ____________
3. ____________
4. ____________
5. ____________
6. ____________
7. ____________
8. ____________
9. ____________
10. ____________
11. ____________
12. ____________
13. ____________

Name____________________

Bonus: List three sets of homonyms that rhyme with *brain*. Example: *Cain, cane*

____________ ____________ ____________

____________ ____________ ____________

Fractured Nursery Rhymes

Can you guess what nursery rhymes the phrases below suggest? Rewrite the sentences on the lines provided.

Example: An egg, perched upon a fence, fell with a thud.

Answer: Humpty Dumpty sat on a wall, Humpty Dumpty had a great fall.

1. A boy and a girl proceeded on a given course, contrary to the natural elevation of land, to get a vessel, commonly circular, of liquid which descends from the clouds.

   Answer: ______________________________

2. A wee lassie has parted with her timid defenseless creatures. She cannot relate in detail at or in what place to come upon by seeking these timid defenseless creatures.

   Answer: ______________________________

3. A miniature, unmarried female child occupied a low seat, munching the coagulated part of milk and the watery part too.

   Answer: ______________________________

Bonus: Make up your own fractured nursery rhyme here.

____

Answer: ______________________________

Name______________________________

The Jones Boys

Mrs. Jones has six boys. The youngest boys are twins. Mike is three times as old as Bob. Allen is three years older than Mike. The oldest son is twelve. Craig is one year younger than Allen. Jason is half the age of Allen. Tom is only three years old and has a twin named Bob.

Use the chart below to figure out the age of each boy.

	Jason age___	**Mike** age___	**Bob** age___	**Craig** age___	**Allen** age___	**Tom** age___
Three-year-old twins						
Is three times as old as Bob						
Is three years older than Bob						
The oldest son is twelve						
Is one year younger than Allen						
Is one half the age of Allen						

Name______________________________

Bonus: When Mike is twice the twins' age, how old will Allen be?

The Fair

Five boys took their animals to the fair. There was a goat, a horse, a rabbit, a hen and a pig. Chris didn't own the goat. Eric rode his animal to the fair, and Adam carried his pet to the fair in a cage. Wally's animal didn't have four legs.

Use the chart below to help you decide which animal belonged to which boy.

	goat				
Chris					
Eric					
Phillip					
Wally					
Adam					

Name____________________________

Bonus: List three boys' names that are also used to mean an animal. Example: *Jack, jack (rabbit)*

Six Cars

Six cars are parked in a row. The red car is directly behind the yellow car. The tan car is fifth in line. The white car is behind the car that is behind the yellow car. The blue car is not the last car. The black car is the second car behind the white car.

Use the chart below to figure out the order of the parked cars.

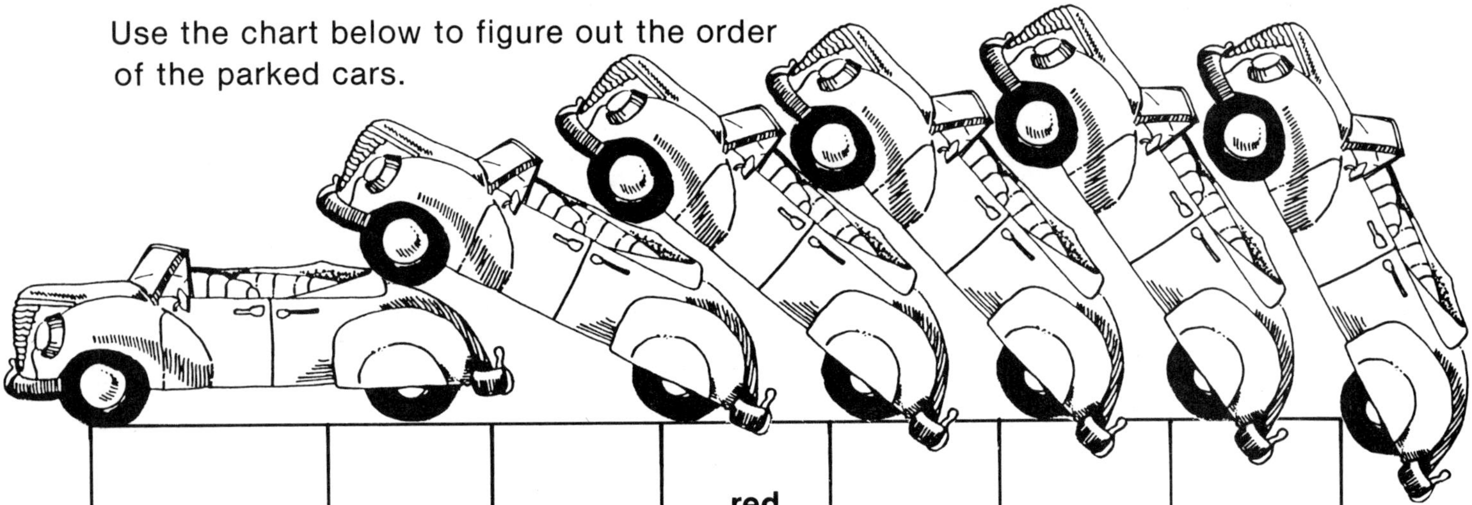

			red			
1st in line						
2nd in line						
3rd in line						
4th in line						
5th in line						
6th in line						

Name_________________________

Bonus: If the black car moves and parks in front of the blue car and the yellow car moves and parks behind the tan car, what color car will be parked behind the third car?

Gold, Gold, Gold!

Before his death, a man named Mr. Silver hid a box of gold coins. He left a clue and stated in his will that the person that solved the clue and found the gold could keep it. Can you decode the message and tell where Mr. Silver hid his gold?

Where is the gold? ____

How did you break the code? ____________________________________

Name ______________________________

Bonus: Some words have numbers or number sounds in them. Write a sentence with six or more words that have number words or number sounds in each word. Example: *Fortunate (4), Tenderfoot (10), ate (8), to (2), fortify (4), wonderful (1), toothaches (2).*

Lunch Out

Six old friends met for lunch. They ate at a round table. Ms. Lucy sat between the nun and the dancer. Ms. Brown is the dancer, and she sat between the singer and Ms. Lucy. The actress sat next to the nun. The nun sat between the teacher and Ms. Jones. Ms. White isn't a writer. Ms. Smith cannot sing a note, but she sat between Ms. David and Ms. Jones, one of which is a singer.

Use the diagram below to figure out where each person sat and give each person's occupation.

Name________________________

Bonus: Which two women could continue working even if they had laryngitis? Explain your answer.

Diamond Thief

You are Detective Marvel. You have a crime to solve. A diamond thief has taken all the jewels from a hotel safe. You know that it had to be the person who came in last. The elevator man can remember the facts found below.

Nancy Blue came in at the stroke of midnight, five minutes before Captain Black. George White came in ten minutes before Mr. Green. Miss Ruby came in thirty minutes before Nancy Blue. Mr. Green did not come in last because he was in by 10:30.

Use the chart below to figure out what time each person came in and who the diamond thief is.

	Nancy Blue				
Came in at midnight	X				

Name____________________________

Bonus: Who came in exactly one hour after Mr. Green? How long was George White home before Mr. Green came home?

____________________________ ____________________________

Picture Message

Below is a message written in words and pictures. Rewrite the message on the lines under the puzzle.

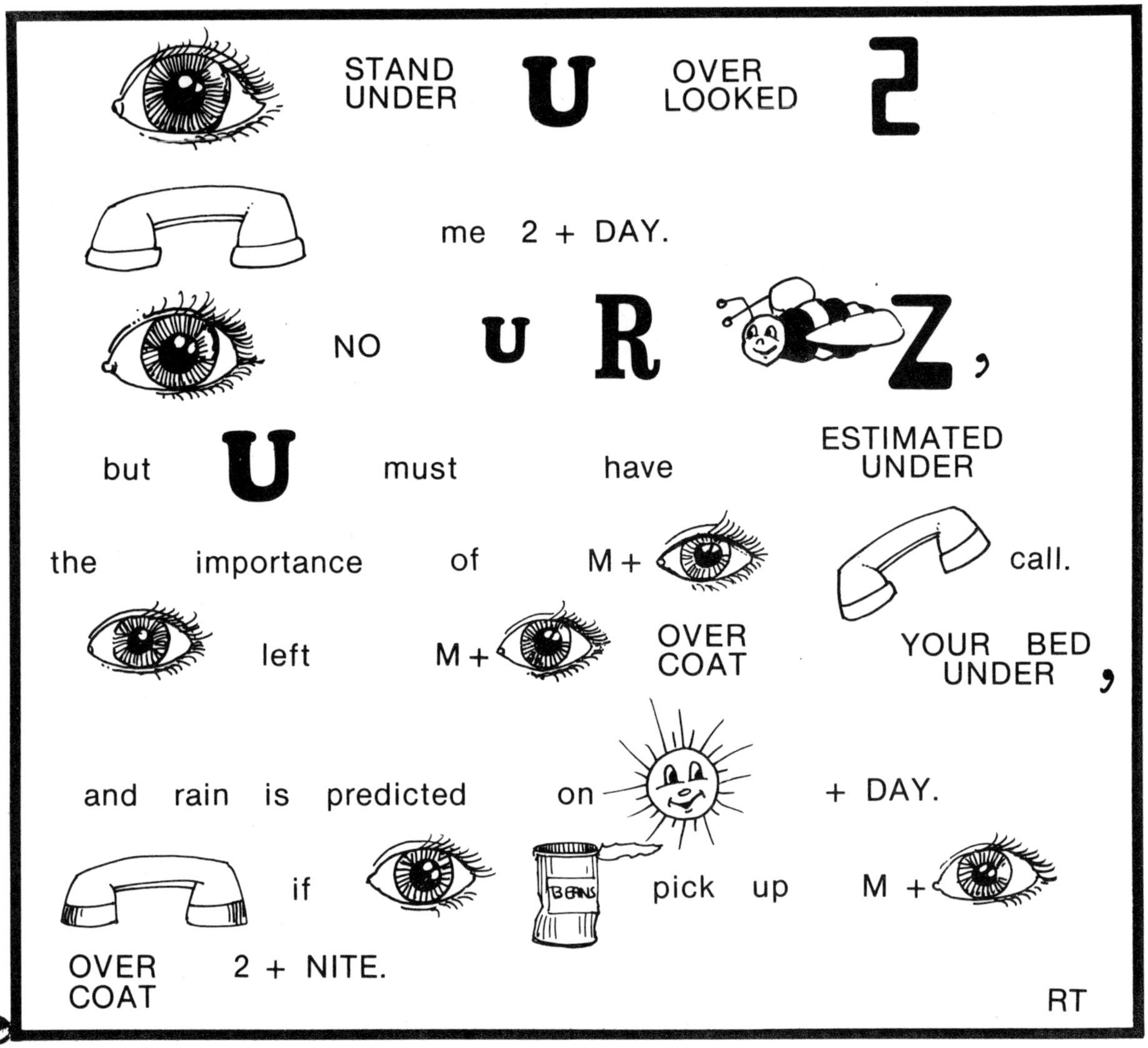

____

____

____

____

____

____

Name______________________________

Bonus: What simple phrase is suggested by the picture?

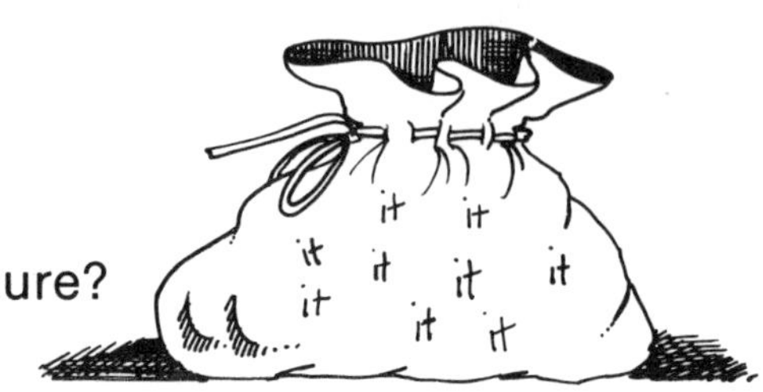

Homonym Hunt

Use a set of homonyms in the blanks to complete each sentence found below.

1. You _______ to _______ the dough a few more minutes.
2. If you live on a ranch and are a _______ you cannot be a _______.
3. The bottom of the _______ was constructed in the shape of an _______.
4. There was so much flooding on our block that the boys _______ a boat down the middle of the _______.
5. _______ fix the broken _______ on your bike if you pay us.
6. He used a _______ as the _______ for his music shop on all his business cards.
7. She couldn't be _______ from buying a _______ jacket.
8. _______ walk down the _______ on my wedding day.
9. When on a diet, it's better to let the cake go to _______ than to your _______.
10. When you _______ for a newspaper, your facts better be _______!

Name_______________________

Bonus: Use a set of three homonyms to complete the sentence found below.

The artist laid his _______ on his _______ and went to the kitchen to find something that would please his _______.

Anagrams Anyone?

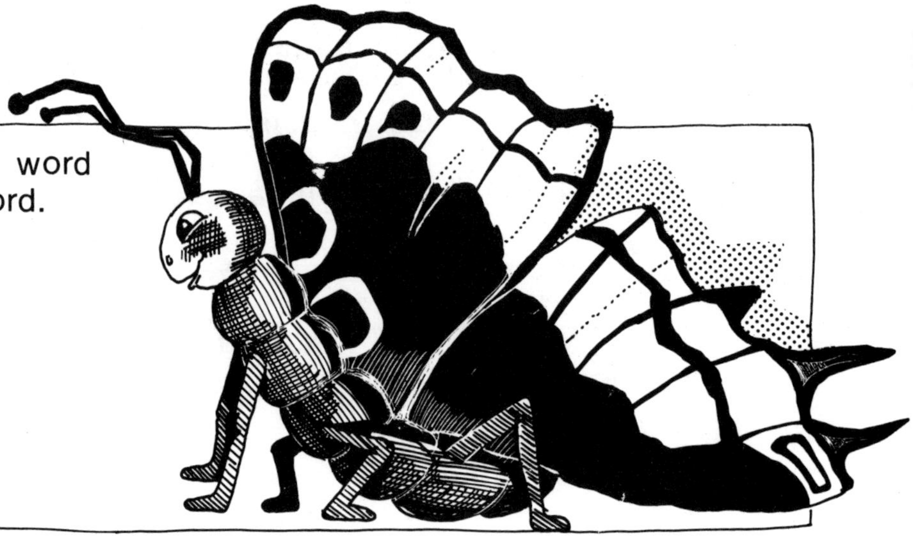

1. Unscramble the letters in each word found below to spell another word.

limped ________

report ________

stream ________

ten ________

2. Unscramble the letters in each word found below to spell two other words.

relay ________ ________

races ________ ________

education ________ ________

bread ________ ________

3. Unscramble the letters in each word found below to spell three other words.

slave ________ ________ ________

notes ________ ________ ________

times ________ ________ ________

cats ________ ________ ________

tables ________ ________ ________

live ________ ________ ________

Bonus: Unscramble the letters in the word *stripe* to spell four other words.

____

____

____

____

Name________________________

Building a Monastery

1. Make a list of eight, two-word combinations using all the letters in the word *monastery*. Example: Mary Stone

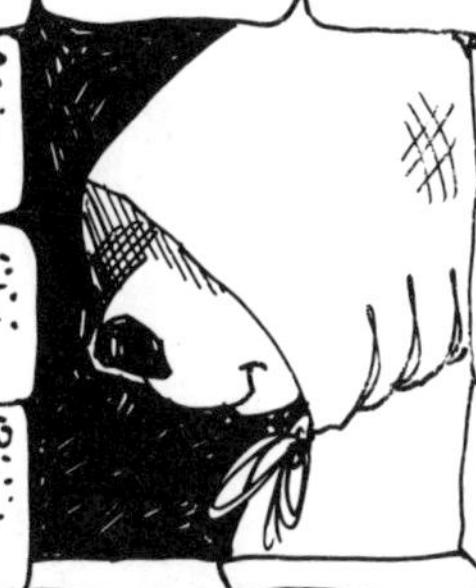

2. Make a list of eight, three-word combinations using all the letters in the word *monastery*. Example: Stay or men

Name____________________________________

Bonus: Make a list of 100 words using only the letters found in *monastery*.

Can It Be?

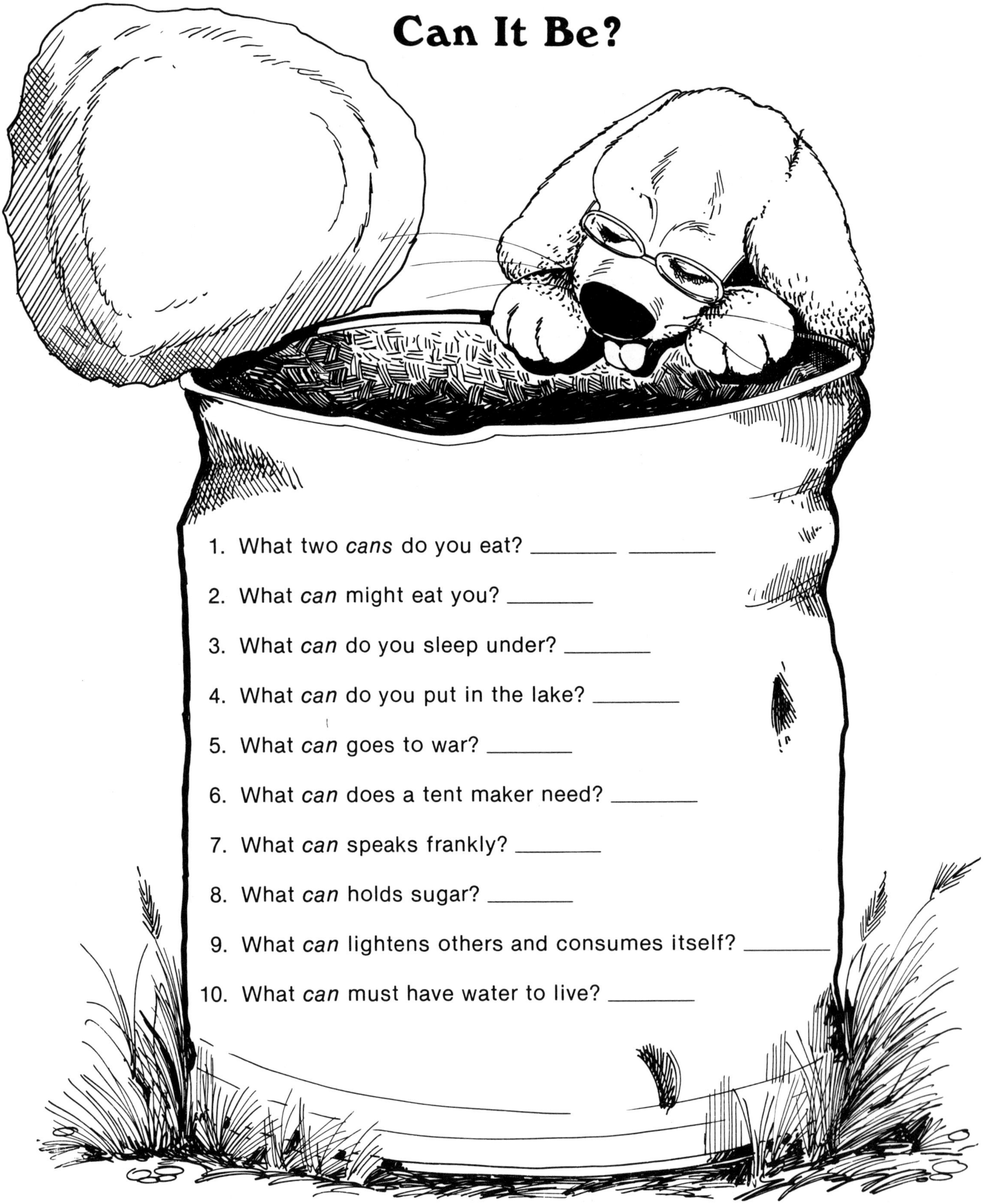

1. What two *cans* do you eat? _______ _______
2. What *can* might eat you? _______
3. What *can* do you sleep under? _______
4. What *can* do you put in the lake? _______
5. What *can* goes to war? _______
6. What *can* does a tent maker need? _______
7. What *can* speaks frankly? _______
8. What *can* holds sugar? _______
9. What *can* lightens others and consumes itself? _______
10. What *can* must have water to live? _______

Name_______________________________

Bonus: What *can* is a nag never without? _______

Teatime

Make a list of twenty words that begin with the letter *T*, and when the letter *T* is dropped, the other letters still spell a word. Example: tone, one

Name____________________________

Bonus: Write a sentence containing at least ten words, each beginning with the letter *T*. The sentence must make sense.

Spoonerism

Spoonerism is the reversing of the first sound of two words in a sentence. Example: A kiss without a moustache is like an egg without salt = A miss without a koustache is like an egg without salt.

Reverse the first sound of two words in each sentence to create famous sayings.

1. I have no fickens and no quarrel with the chox.

   ____

2. No trope is strong enough to hang the Ruth.

   ____

3. One cloud is enough so hide the tun.

   ____

4. A chood bird begins girping in the egg.

   ____

5. A bad bustom's like a good cake, better croken.

   ____

6. Through a small sole one can see the hky.

   ____

7. A man cannot thistle and drink at the same wime.

   ____

8. He cannot weak spell that cannot hold his tongue.

   ____

9. The boon does not heed the marking of the dogs.

   ____

10. Step after step the cladder is limbed.

    ____

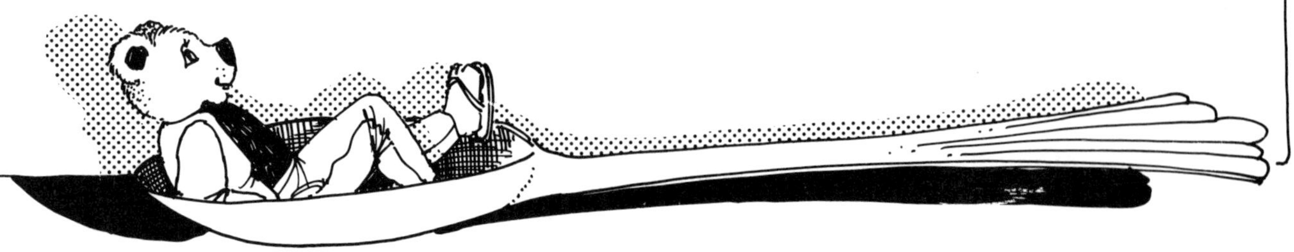

Name______________________________

Bonus: Think of a famous saying. Reverse two of the initial sounds to create a spoonerism.

____

____

Color Your Words

Some words have colors as part of the word. Example: This is a black and white TV. 

Color the words found below so that each one represents a word with a color in its name.

Name______________________________

Bonus: Use another sheet of paper to think up other words that have color words in them. Design a puzzle like this one for your parents or friends.

Where Are You From?

Use the name of a state to answer each of the questions. Your answer should be as clever as the question. Example: What does Connecticut (Con Nety cut) with? An Arkansas (Ark an' saw)

1. What does Delaware (Dela wear)? ____________________
2. What does Tennessee (Tenny see)? ____________________
3. What does Iowa (I.O. weigh)? ____________________
4. Where has Oregon (Ory gone)? ____________________
5. What did Idaho (Ida hoe)? ____________________
6. What did Mississippi (Missy sippy)? ____________________

Name____________________

Bonus: Write your own zany state questions, but make sure your questions have good answers.

Scrambled Sayings

Unscramble the words found in each sentence below to discover some famous sayings.

1. A nyenp vsdea si a nyenp nraeed.

2. lAl loeepp miles ni eth meas gageulna.

3. heT rleay drbi segt het mwor.

4. A tischt ni imte veass ienn.

5. Teh lkim of manuh ssnnkdie reven culserd.

6. onHtesy si laawys het ebst oicypl.

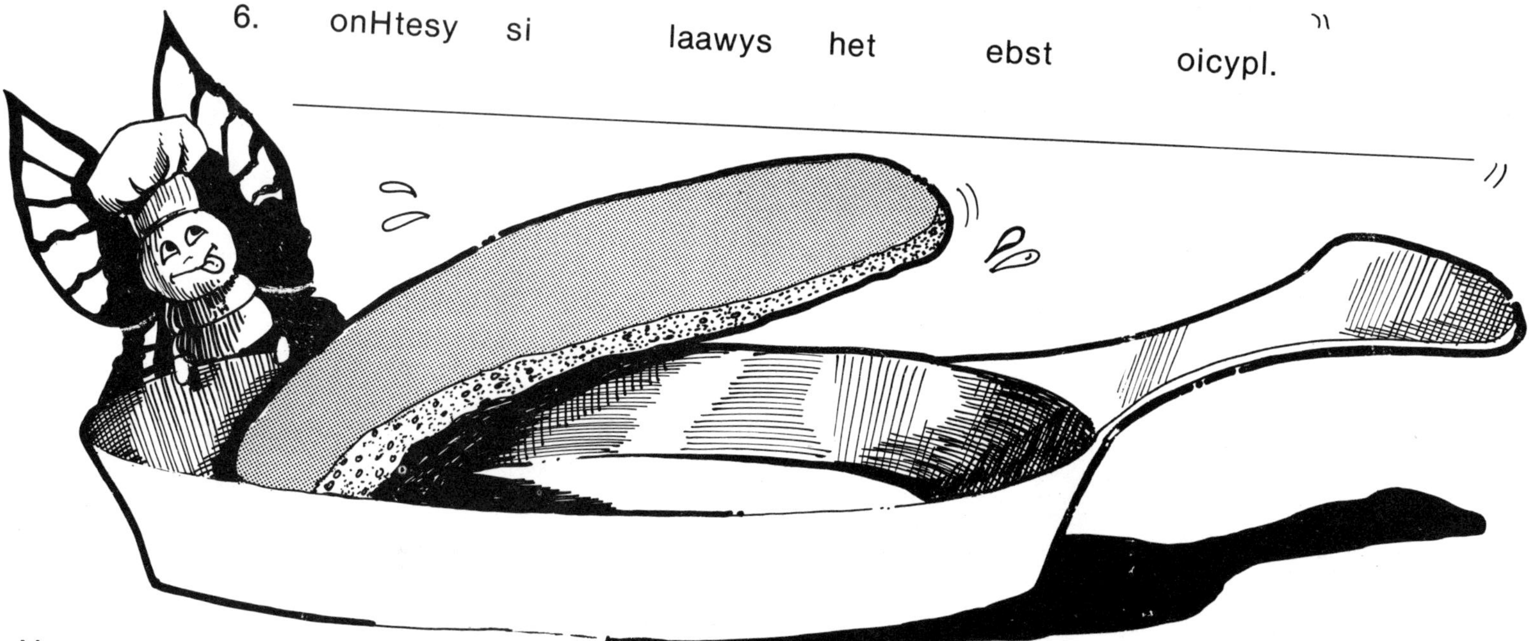

Name______________________________

Bonus: Can you think of an animal that begins with double A's? Double L's? Double E's?

Vowels Needed!

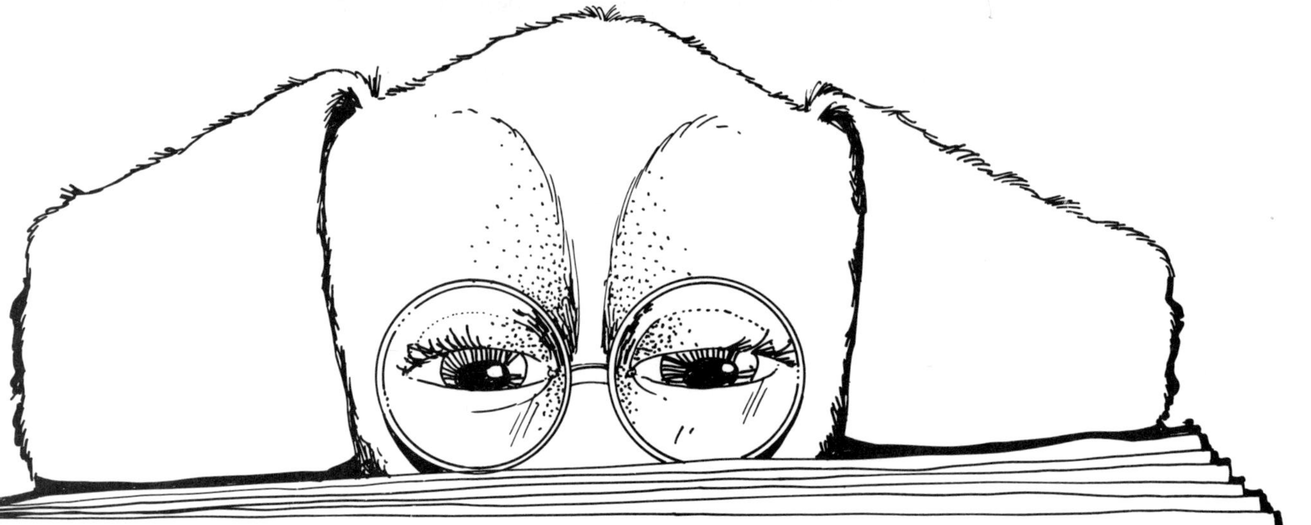

Add a vowel one or more times to each row of letters found below to form words. Example: hrss = harass

1. bliv ______
2. prphernli ______
3. pprel ______
4. tbggan ______
5. trtise ______
6. psychlgy ______
7. htrognous ______
8. etble ______
9. nsatable ______
10. sovrign ______
11. xylphne ______
12. Msssspp ______

Name______

Bonus: What two letters are not found in any two-letter state abbreviations? What vowel and what letter are found the most in the two-letter state abbreviations?

______ ______

Create Your Own Chart

Fill in the top three boxes with topics. Example: fruits, animals, musical instruments, games, boys' names, etc. Then complete the chart by filling in the words that begin with the appropriate letters and belong in the appropriate columns.

A			
B			
C			
D			
E			
F			
G			
H			
I			
J			
K			
L			
M			
N			
O			
P			
Q			
R			
S			
T			
U			
V			
W			
X			
Y			
Z			

Name________________________

Bonus: Can you choose topics so that you can fill in every blank in the chart?

Answer Key

Patterns Page 1
1. N (every other letter)
2. V (letters that follow vowels)
3. U (skip 1, skip 2, skip 3, etc.)
4. R (capital letters with curves)
5. Y (capital letters formed with 3 straight lines and no curves)

Bonus: typewriter

Simple Phrases Page 2
1. go to the dogs
2. have an axe to grind
3. paint the town red
4. bite the dust
5. knee-high to a grasshopper

Remove One Page 3
1. Mary, Jack
2. horse, colt
3. chair, kitchen
4. Tuesday, May
5. Roy, baseball
6. corn, rose

Bonus: bookkeeper

Word Towers Page 4
Answers will vary.
O, on, ton, tone, stone, stones
A, an, ran, rain, train, strain
E, we, wee, weep, sweep, sweeps
I, in, pin, spin, spine, spines
Bonus: sprint, print, pint, pin, in, I

Gals and Lads Page 5
1. galaxy
2. gala
3. gallery
4. Galileo
5. galore

1. lady
2. ladder
3. ladybug
4. ladle
5. laden

Bonus: galoshes, lady's slipper

Mix and Match Proverbs Page 6
1. e, 2. f, 3. a, 4. b, 5. g, 6. h, 7. c, 8. d, 9. l, 10. k, 11. j, 12. i, 13. o, 14. m, 15. n
Bonus: When a friend asks, there is no tomorrow.

Sky High Page 7
Answers will vary.
amplify, by, cry, die, eye, fly, guy, high, intensify, July, knee-high, lie, my, nigh, outcry, pie, qualify, rye, shy, tie, unify, vie, why, xi, yarn-dye
Bonus: multiply, July

Sentence Fun Page 8
1. Oh, I see you.
2. I see a bee.
3. Are you Jay?
4. I have to be in by ten.
5. Are you late too?
6. I won a tin teacup.
7. I see an Indian tepee.
8. Am I too late to see Jay?

1. EZ (easy)
2. NME (enemy)
3. RT (Arty), J (Jay)
4. XS (excess)

Answers will vary.
Bonus: XLNC

Who Is It? Page 9
1. Washington
2. Einstein
3. Beethoven
4. Thomas Edison
5. Patrick Henry
6. Thomas Jefferson

Bonus: I overlooked the newspaper this morning.

Antonym Phrases Page 10
1. fly off the handle
2. keep tabs on
3. bark up the wrong tree
4. pass the buck
5. bury the hatchet
6. It won't hold water.

Bonus: Justice is truth in action.

Throw One Out! Page 11
Answers will vary.
1. tomato (others grow underground)
2. circle (others have corners)
3. dice (others are round)
4. hen (others have four legs)
5. tomato (others are orange)
6. tree (others you can open)

Bonus: Private? No! Children allowed.

Scrambled Eggs Page 12
1. rain, reign
2. guessed, guest
3. night, knight
4. boughs, bows
5. crooked, straight
6. beautiful, ugly
7. young, old
8. awake, asleep
9. build, construct
10. blame, accuse
11. meander, wander
12. tote, transport

Bonus: bear, bare; bee, be; boar, bore; boy, buoy; castor, caster; chough, chuff; deer, dear; doe, dough; does, doze; ewe, you; fawn, faun; flea, flee; fowl, foul; grizzly, grisly; hare, hair; hart, heart; horse, hoarse; nag, knag; gnu, knew; leech, leach; lynx, links; martin, marten; mule, mewl; mite, might; otter, ottar; rabbit, rabbet; roes, rows, rose; roe, row; cygnet, signet; tapir, taper; ewes, yews, use; whale, wail, wale

Once Again Page 13
1. The horizon is not the boundary of the world.
2. See no evil; hear no evil; speak no evil.
3. The secret of success is hard work.
4. Money is a good servant but a poor master.
5. The virtue lies in the struggle, not in the prize.
6. Waste not, want not.
7. To be or not to be, that is the question.

Bonus: You cannot make an omelet without breaking eggs.

Syllable Riddles Page 14
1. earth + quake = earthquake
2. mitt + ten = mitten
3. L + bow = elbow
4. spin + stir = spinster
5. sweep + steak = sweepstake

Bonus: When it is slapstick (slap + stick).

Anagrams Page 15
1. limped
2. wards
3. parted
4. report
5. stream, tamers
6. steals, tassel
7. post, tops, pots
8. relay
9. veil, live, vile
10. stone, tones
11. rates, tears
12. reaps, spear
13. pot
14. meat, mate
15. items, mites, emits
16. cuter, truce

Bonus: stop: tops, spot, post, pots

Rhymes Page 16
1. obese
2. antique
3. celebrate
4. design
5. utilize
6. dough
7. tear
8. zigzag
9. excel

Bonus: blab, crab, dab, drab, grab

Rhyming Chart Page 17
Answers will vary.
am, ram, yam, slam
dill, whippoorwill, daffodil, shrill
nine, swine, pine, whine
tape, ape, grape, scrape
air, bear, pear, blare

Bonus: bee, flea; cat, gnat, rat, bat; quail, whale; drake, snake; shrimp, chimp; dog, hog, frog; doe, crow, buffalo; bug, slug; roe, crow

Answer Key

Search and Circle Page 18

1. oppose, comply
2. continue, cease
3. seize, release
4. serene, disturbed

1. scarce, rare
2. hasty, sudden
3. swell, expand
4. coarse, rough

Bonus: segregate, separate

Go Search! page 19

1. a, at, ate, I, rate, irate, pirate, pirates, rates, rain, in, train, strain, rat
2. I, in, pin, pins, spin, spins, turnip, turnips, nip, nips, turn, urn, spinster

Bonus: The misspelled word is *misspelled*.

Alphabetical Words Page 20

Answers will vary.

abet, abhor, abort, ace, adept, adz, aim, air, airy, am, an, ant, apt, art, ary, as, at, ax, be, beg, begin, belt, bent, bet, bin, blow, bop, bow, buy, by, cent, chil, chin, chimp, copy, deft, defy, deny, dip, film, ghost, him, hop, host, knot, know, lost, mop, most

Bonus: daffodil, whippoorwill

Big and Little Page 21

1. large
2. extensive
3. vast
4. immense
5. enormous
6. tremendous
7. huge
8. massive
9. gigantic
10. mammoth

1.	week	second
2.	day	minute
3.	second	evening
4.	month	day
5.	minute	week
6.	season	month
7.	year	season
8.	evening	year
9.	decade	decade
10.	century	century

Bonus: minute (min´it) (mi noot´)

Synonym Acrostics Page 22

1. convert, shift, transform, turn, exchange, alter
2. expel, nudge, shove, thrust
3. exasperation, irritation, rage, vexation, fury
4. pick, tug, haul, pluck

Bonus: catastrophe, calamity

A Place to Dwell Page 23

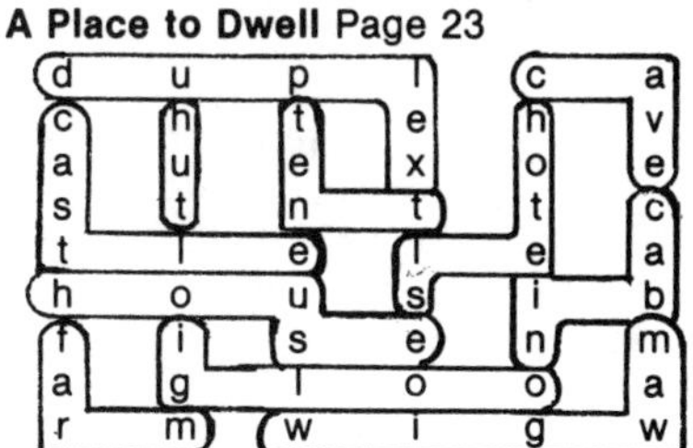

Bonus: London

Double Letter Zoo Page 24

1. gorilla
2. gazelle
3. squirrel
4. goose
5. moose
6. buffalo
7. giraffe
8. hippopotamus
9. opossum
10. rabbit
11. reindeer

Bonus: orangutan (orange + tan, change E to U)

Fifty Cents Worth Page 25

Answers will vary.

absent, accident, acknowledgment, bent, cement, comment, competent, complement, confident, consent, content, continent, dent, detriment, different, dissent, document, element, eloquent, event, evident, excellent, extent, ferment, frequent, government, incident, innocent, instrument, lent, management, meant, monument, negligent, nourishment, nutrient, nutriment, orient, ornament, president, punishment, relent, rent, resident, scent, sent, settlement, spent, tent, vent, violent, went

Bonus: compliment, complement

Ring One Out Page 26

1. bad
2. genuine
3. rise
4. pull
5. grand
6. close
7. beef
8. terrible
9. ordinary
10. unknown
11. vanish
12. doubt
13. hide
14. idleness

Bonus: prompt (others are misspelled)

Synonym Squares Page 27

1. lope
   o d
   a g
   dine
2. rare
   e v
   a e
   lawn
3. group
   r l
   e u
   a c
   think

Thinker Sheet Page 28

1. raise, raze, rays
2. cat, rat, bat, gnat
3. danger
4. pessimistic
5. mysterious
6. opaque
7. Maine—mane, main
8. Answers will vary.
   watch, itch, match, witch, catch, pitch, patch, latch, stretch, crutch, stitch, hitch
9. Answers will vary.
   knot, knit, know, knead, knuckle, knack, knight, knee, knew, knob, knife, kneel, knock

Bonus: claustrophobia

Figuratively Speaking Page 29

1. jump the gun
2. eat humble pie
3. upset the apple cart
4. a wet blanket
5. take the cake
6. beat the band
7. pleased as punch

1. a wild goose chase
2. to beat the band
3. bark up the wrong tree
4. play second fiddle
5. jump the gun
6. once in a blue moon

Bonus: More power to you.

In Your Own Words Page 30

1. . . . never expect to gather roses.
2. . . . to those that do them good.
3. . . . adulation, fawning and flattery.
4. . . . rather talkative.
5. . . . a silly laugh.
6. . . . more lasting than bronze.
7. . . . groves academe.
8. . . . the doom of beauty.
9. . . . be lovable.
10. . . . everybody.
11. . . . that is poor.
12. . . . a great slavery.

Letter Fun Page 31

Answers will vary.

1. M (turns ice to mice)
2. U (always in the middle of fun)
3. G (always in the middle of night)
4. Y (makes pa pay)
5. A (in the middle of day)
6. F (capital of France)
7. T (at the end of the alphabet)

Bonus: The letter *E*

Animal Parade Page 32

Answers will vary.

Bonus: whippoorwill

Answer Key

A Long Vacation Page 33
Answers will vary.
Bonus: Tennessee, Mississippi

Hidden Girls and Boys Page 34
Answers will vary.
Sarah, Mary, Amy, Ruth, Anna, Jane, Sue, Jenny, Karen, Ann
Tom, Terry, Jerry, Joe, Jack, John, Tim, Henry, Harry
Bonus: Ann, an; Bea, be; Cain, cane; Carole, carol; Frank, franc; Lee, lea; Mark, marque; Marshall, martial; Martin, marten; Pearl, purl

Associations Page 35
1. box
2. super
3. ship
4. foot
5. pine
6. sun

Bonus: white

Brain Strain Page 36
Answers will vary.
Cain, cane, chain, drain, rain, gain, grain, lain, mane, main, pain, plain, plane
Bonus: lain, lane; reign, rain; vain, vane; wain, wane

Fractured Nursery Rhymes Page 37
1. Jack and Jill went up the hill to fetch a pail of water.
2. Little Bo-Peep has lost her sheep and can't tell where to find them.
3. Little Miss Muffet sat on a tuffet, eating her curds and whey.

The Jones Boys Page 38
Allen is 12; Craig is 11; Mike is 9; Jason is 6; Bob and Tom are 3.
Bonus: In three years Mike will be 12, the twins will be 6 and Allen will be 15.

The Fair Page 39
Adam, rabbit; Phillip, goat; Chris, pig; Eric, horse; Wally, hen
Bonus: Jay (bird), Martin (bird), Morgan (horse), Tom (turkey or cat)

Six Cars Page 40
1. blue, 2. yellow, 3. red, 4. white, 5. tan, 6. black
Bonus: white

Gold, Gold, Gold! Page 41
Message: In the attic (Cross out the word *gold* three times in the message.)

Lunch Out Page 42
Lucy, teacher; Brown, dancer; David, singer; Smith, writer; Jones, actress; White, nun
Bonus: Brown, Smith (A dancer and a writer could do their work without using their voices.)

Diamond Thief Page 43
George White, 10:20; Mr. Green, 10:30; Miss Ruby 11:30, Nancy Blue, 12:00; Captain Black, 12:05. Captain Black is the thief.
Bonus: Miss Ruby, 10 minutes

Picture Message Page 44
I understand you overlooked to phone me today. I know you are busy, but you must have underestimated the importance of my phone call. I left my overcoat under your bed, and rain is predicted on Sunday. Phone if I can pick up my overcoat tonight.

Arty.

Bonus: It's in the bag.

Homonym Hunt Page 45
1. need, knead
2. coward, cowherd
3. ark, arc
4. rowed, road
5. We'll, wheel
6. cymbal, symbol
7. swayed, suede
8. I'll, aisle
9. waste, waist
10. write, right

Bonus: palette, pallet, palate

Anagrams Anyone? Page 46
1. limped, dimple; report, porter; stream, master; ten, net
2. relay, layer, early; races, cares, scare; education, cautioned, auctioned; bread, bared, beard
3. slave, vales, salve, veals
   notes, tones, stone, onset
   times, items, smite, mites, emits
   cats, scat, acts, cast
   tables, stable, bleats, ablest
   live, evil, Levi, veil, vile

Bonus: stripe—sprite, tripes, esprit, ripest

Building a Monastery Page 47
1. nasty Rome, stony mare, mean story, my senator, many store, money arts, my treason, no mastery
2. no arms yet, seam try on, no rye mats, on rye mats, my one star, on mars yet, nor mat yes

Bonus: a, an, am, are, arm, arms, as, ant, ants, art, arts at, ate, eat, eats, man, mare, men, many, money, moneys, mastery, mean, means, mat, mats, me, may, mart, marts, nest, nasty, note, notes, name, names, nor, on, or, ore, one, ran, ram, ray, rat, rats, rams, rays, rest, rye, rate, rates, ream, reams, son, some, stone, stony, sat, set, stay, steam, stream, star, stary, sane, senator, same, store, smart, so, stern, seam, seams, ten, ton, tan, tame, tone, tones, to, term, terms, tans, team, teams, tray, trays, tar, tore, tear, tears, treason, try, tries, year, years, yen, yet, yes

Can It Be? Page 48
1. cantelope and candy
2. cannibal
3. canopy
4. canoe
5. cannon
6. canvas
7. candor
8. canister
9. candle
10. canal

Bonus: canter

Teatime Page 49
tape, tart, tale, taunt, tease, tend, that, thick, then, this, thug, true, those, terror, train, trappings, trusty, trash, trifle, trend, tweed

Spoonerism Page 50
1. I have no chickens and no quarrel with the fox.
2. No rope is strong enough to hang the truth.
3. One cloud is enough to hide the sun.
4. A good bird begins chirping in the egg.
5. A bad custom's like a good cake, better broken.
6. Through a small hole one can see the sky.
7. A man cannot whistle and drink at the same time.
8. He cannot speak well that cannot hold his tongue.
9. The moon does not heed the barking of the dogs.
10. Step after step the ladder is climbed.

Color Your Words Page 51
red hot, gray V = gravy, black top, blacksmith or silversmith, brown E = brownie or silver E = silvery, White House or greenhouse, Purple Heart, yellow jacket, orange (orange), green thumb, green pepper

Where Are You From? Page 52
1. A New Jersey (new jersey)
2. The same thing that Arkansas (Ark Ann saw).
3. She weighs a Washington (Wash 'nd ton).
4. She has gone to Oklahoma (Okla's homa).
5. She hoed a Maryland (merry land).
6. She sipped a Minnesota (mini soda).

Scrambled Sayings Page 53
1. A penny saved is a penny earned.
2. All people smile in the same language.
3. The early bird gets the worm.
4. A stitch in time saves nine.
5. The milk of human kindness never curdles.
6. Honesty is always the best policy.

Bonus: aardvark, llama, eel

Vowels Needed! Page 54
1. believe
2. paraphernalia
3. apparel
4. toboggan
5. tortoise
6. psychology
7. heterogeneous
8. eatable
9. insatiable
10. sovereign
11. xylophone
12. Mississippi

Bonus: B and Q, A = 12 times, N = 11 times

Bonus Award Certificate

To ______________________________

From ____________________________

Word Puzzle Expert!

To ________________

____

From ____________

____

Synonym Super Star

To ______________

____

From ______________

____

Homonym Hound

To ______________

____

From ______________

____

Antonym Award

To ______________

____

From ______________

____

Outstanding Effort Award

To ______________

From ______________